# PIRATES

Written by Paul Stevenson

# CONTENTS

First published in 2026 by
Hungry Tomato Ltd
F15, Old Bakery Studios, Blewetts Wharf, Malpas Road,
Truro, Cornwall, TR1 1QH, UK.

Thanks to our editor, Julie Tofflemire.





A CIP catalog record for this book is available from the
British Library.

ISBN 9781835694480

Manufactured in the USA

Discover more at
www.hungrytomato.com

All words in **BOLD** can be found in the glossary.

# THIEVES ABOARD!

Bold, adventurous, and tough, pirates sailed the seas, hunting ships for treasure.

Thieves on the water have been around for thousands of years. But in the sixteenth century, major trade routes opened up between Europe and the Far East.

Ships filled with gold and silver sailed the Indian Ocean, offering chances for pirates to make lots of money.

But would the rewards be worth the risk?

# A PIRATE'S LIFE

**Life as a pirate was never easy. Surviving – and succeeding – meant having to face enormous challenges.**

Battles at sea were hard work as well as very dangerous. When pirates set out on their adventures, they never knew if they would be coming back safely.

For those who got caught by pirate hunters or **naval fleets**, it could mean **imprisonment** or even death!

The ocean can be unpredictable and harsh. Rough seas could damage the ship, sometimes destroying it completely.

Sickness and **disease** spread easily on the ship. With limited supplies on board, it was difficult to treat illnesses and injuries.

# READY TO FIGHT

**Pirates used a variety of weapons to defend themselves... and to attack others!**

Cannon could damage the enemy ship's sails, masts, and **hull**. They were also used for firing warning shots to scare other crews.

Guns were popular weapons with pirates, but they weren't always useful. When the sea was choppy, aiming guns accurately could be difficult, and reloading took a long time.

The cutlass sword was used frequently, thanks to its short blade. This made it easier to fight in tight spaces.

Daggers could be hidden in clothes for surprise attacks. In the **cutthroat** pirate world, you always had to be ready to fight!

# LIFE AT SEA

**When on their ship, pirates had no privacy, and they often faced a lack of supplies.**

Only the captain had private **quarters**. Crew members slept in open areas on the floor or in **hammocks**.

There were no showers, so pirates washed when it rained or took a dip in the sea.

What about bathroom breaks? Captains might have had a **chamber pot**, but everyone else had to go right on **deck**! They used a platform with a hole in it.

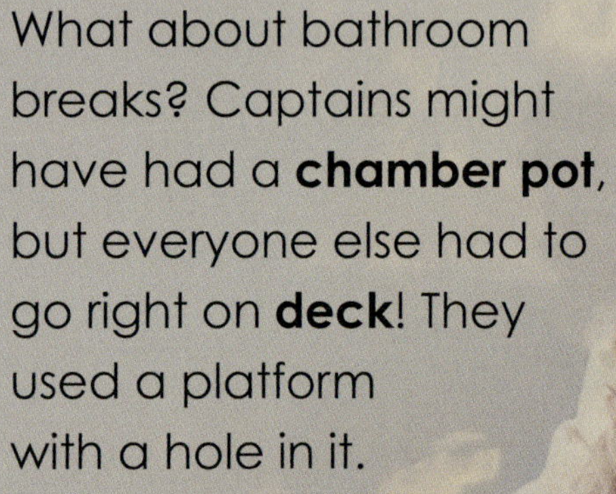

Hammocks

A pirate's diet
was not healthy.
The main foods
were dried meat,
which was difficult
to chew, and
hardtack, a thick
cracker made
from flour, water,
and salt.

Hardtack

Without the vitamin C in fresh fruit and vegetables, many
pirates suffered from scurvy, a disease that could kill.

Sometimes pirates had to eat rotten food when supplies ran
low. Even worse – in 1671, one pirate crew had to eat roasted
leather **satchels**!

# KEEPING THE CODE

**Life at sea offered certain freedoms, but pirates couldn't always do whatever they wanted.**

Most ships had their own code of conduct that the crew had to follow. The code often included rules about **gambling** and also banned women from going aboard the ship!

The pirate code ruled that all treasure must be shared among the crew. However, the captain and other high-ranking pirates usually got a bigger share.

There were tough punishments for anyone who broke the pirate code.

**Flogging** was common, and sometimes sailors were sent to the crow's nest for long periods.

A pirate sentenced to death on board could be made to "walk the plank" into the sea, but this was rare.

Usually, **condemned** pirates were shot, or thrown from high up in the **rigging** onto the deck.

# SHIPSHAPE

**A strong and seaworthy ship was essential for success, so the crew had to take good care of it.**

When the ship was at sea, regular repairs were necessary to stop water from getting in.

Using a caulking iron, the gaps or seams between the **planks** were filled with small pieces of rope and then sealed with **tar**.

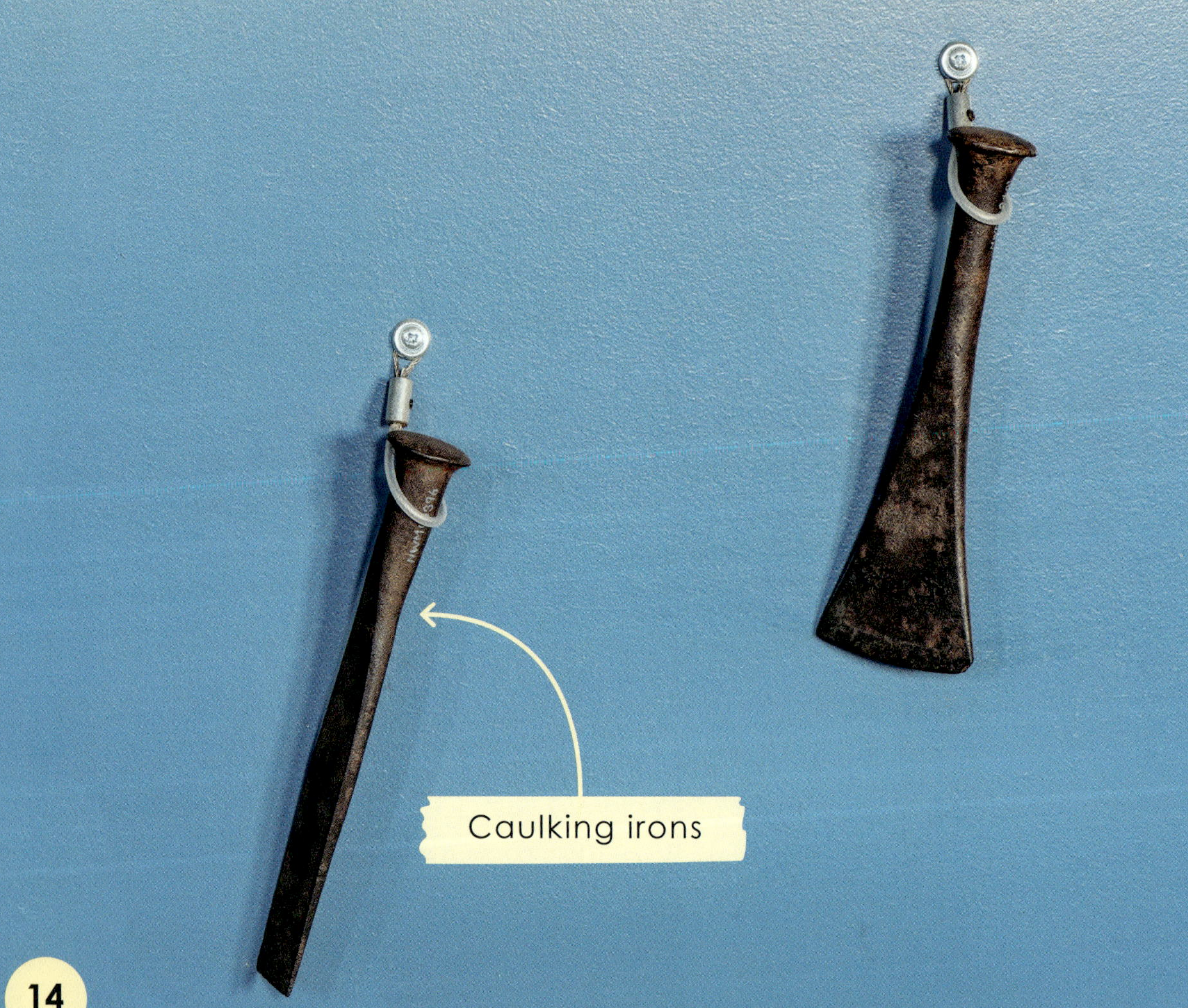

Caulking irons

Crew members had to regularly "swab the deck" - that is, clean it with a mop.

The hull also needed cleaning every few months, as barnacles and seaweed slowed the ship down. To do this, the ship was pulled onto the sand at low tide. This was very dangerous as it left the ship exposed to attack!

# LEGAL THEFT

**Governments sometimes allowed, or even encouraged, pirate activities.**

Privateers were pirates who worked for a government. If a country was at war with another, it would **license** a shipowner to attack the enemy's **vessels** in return for a share of the **booty**.

**Licenses** given to privateers were called "letters of marque".

They allowed sailors to attack enemies and not be charged with piracy themselves.

These licenses were helpful before a country had set up a navy. Later, some countries tried to stop privateering because sailors preferred it to joining the navy!

A letter of marque from 1618 (license)

# SUPER STRATEGIES

**Pirates had clever ways to help them get the treasure they wanted.**

Timing was everything! Attacking at night was a way to take the enemy by surprise.

Treasure ships were often attacked at the beginning of a trip. That's because they couldn't gain much speed until they found a strong wind to power the sails.

Fear could be a powerful weapon too. A reputation for ruthlessness could make people **surrender** before the battle even began.

Privateer Jonathan Haraden once threatened to attack a ship by standing next to a cannon, holding a burning candle. The ship surrendered, not knowing Jonathan only had one cannonball!

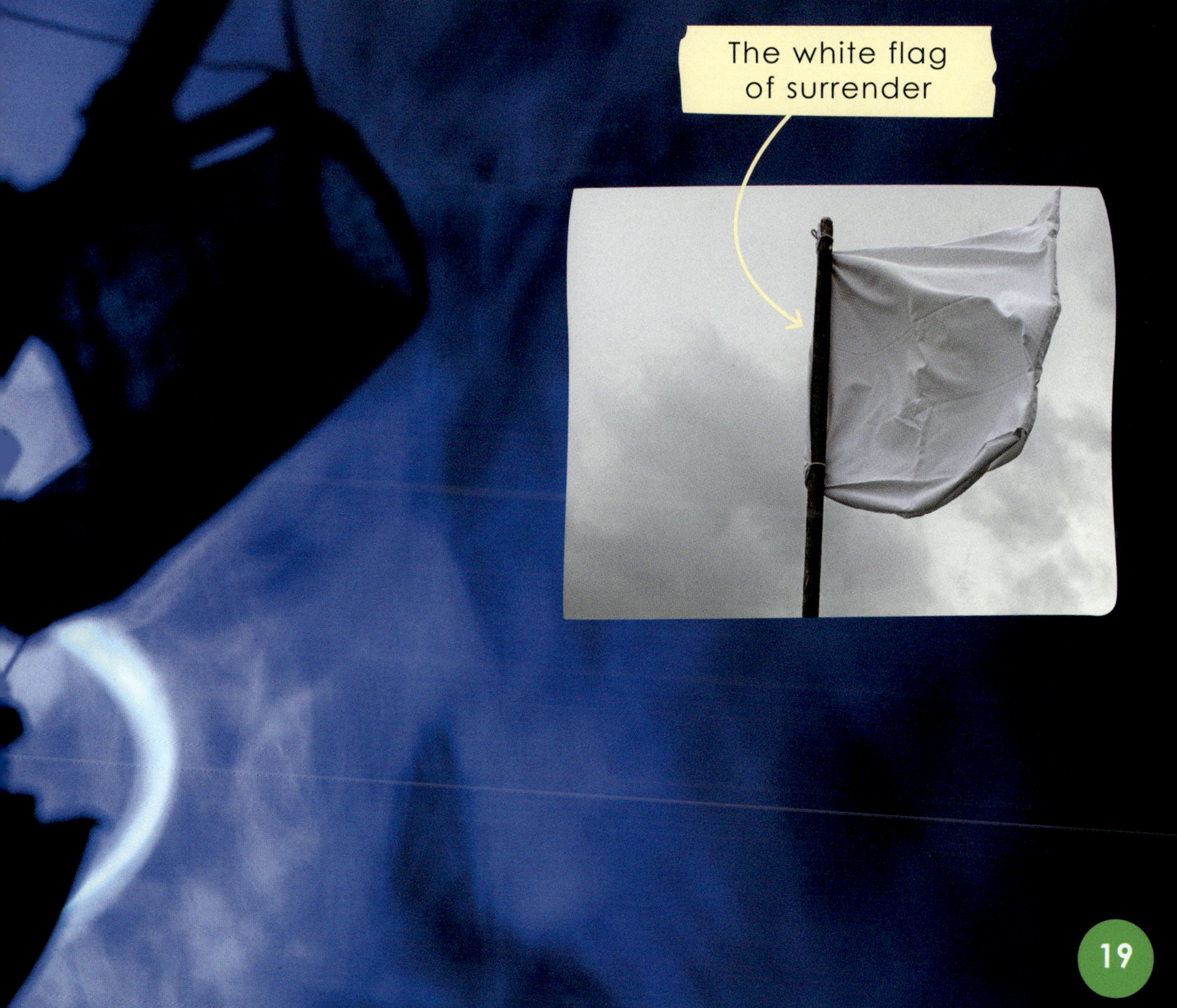

# THE GOLDEN AGE

**During the "Golden Age of Piracy" (1680-1718), fearsome captains ruled the seas.**

Edward Teach (1680-1718), better known as Blackbeard, terrorized the waters off the North American coast.

He made himself look even more terrifying by tying smoking fuses under his hat to surround himself with smoke!

Legend has it that Blackbeard even harmed some of his own crew members to maintain his scary reputation.

Henry Morgan (1635-1688) led many daring raids on ships and towns owned by the Spanish. King Charles II was so impressed that he made Morgan Deputy Governor of Jamaica.

King Charles II

Henry Morgan

William Kidd (1645-1701), also called Captain Kidd, started off as a privateer. But when he didn't capture any ships for a long time, he decided to turn to piracy. Bad move! He was eventually put to death for his crimes!

Captain Kidd

# WARRIOR WOMEN

**Most ships were only crewed by men as it was considered bad luck to have women on board. This didn't stop women who wanted to sail the high seas!**

Anne Bonny (around 1698-1782) became a pirate after meeting Captain "Calico Jack" Rackham in the Bahamas.

Together, the pair raided Spanish treasure ships until they were captured in 1720.

Mary Read (1695-1721) also joined Jack Rackham's pirate crew. But unlike Anne Bonny, she disguised herself as a man. Read was a fearless fighter – only she and Anne Bonny fought back when Rackham's ship was captured by the British navy!

Charlotte De Berry joined the British navy, pretending to be a man. When she was attacked by her captain, she led a **rebellion** against him and cut off his head. Charlotte took command and the crew became pirates.

# NO SEA WAS SAFE!

**The Caribbean sea, North African coast, and Indian Ocean were hotspots for pirates. But piracy happened all over the world.**

More than a thousand years ago, fearsome Viking pirates began to attack parts of northern Europe.

The Vikings had longships that could carry up to 50 people. They used **oars** to row the boats swiftly to the shore.

Zheng Yi Sao

In the nineteenth century, a woman called Zheng Yi Sao inherited a huge pirate empire from her husband. She controlled a fleet of 400 ships, which attacked vessels off the coast of China.

In the Persian Gulf, Rahmah bin Jabr set light to the gunpowder store on his ship to avoid capture by rival pirates. He blew himself up, but also destroyed half of the attacking ships!

# WHAT A HAUL!

**Why did people become pirates? To make their fortunes, of course!**

In 1693, the American pirate Thomas Tew overpowered a ship returning to Bombay. The vessel was packed with booty, and members of Tew's crew received enormous shares, worth more than they could each earn over 90 years in a regular job!

A famous haul was made by Henry Avery (also known as Henry Every) in 1695. He captured a Mughal ship that was carrying precious metals and jewels worth the equivalent of $145 million (£115 million) in today's money!

A generous prize was offered for Avery's capture, leading to the first ever global search for a criminal.

# PIRATE FLAGS

**Pirates used flags to identify themselves, intimidate other sailors, and trick them.**

The flag of a pirate ship, known as the Jolly Roger, was anything but jolly! Perhaps the most common design was the skull and crossbones, but this wasn't the only pirate flag!

A Jolly Roger with cross swords

The earliest pirate flags were plain red, the color of blood! They sent a chilling signal to other crews – no mercy would be given.

Christopher Moody's flag

Blackbeard's flag showed a skeleton aiming a spear at a bleeding heart. The figure also held an hourglass, showing sailors that their time had run out!



Pirates sometimes tricked enemy ships by flying a "friendly" flag. As the pirates drew close, they would suddenly raise the Jolly Roger just before they started the attack! Each pirate had their own Jolly Roger flag.

Thomas Tew's flag

Henry Avery's flag

# MODERN-DAY PIRATES

**Pirates don't just belong in history books!**

**What do modern-day pirates steal?**
- Merchandise from cargo ships
- Oil from tanker ships
- The entire ship!

**How to stop modern-day pirates**
- Water cannon to keep pirate boats away
- Sharp razor wire to make it difficult to board the boat
- Guards on the vessel to protect the crew and property

# GLOSSARY

**booty** – valuable things that are stolen, especially by pirates or soldiers.

**chamber pot** – a round container kept in a bedroom and used as a toilet.

**condemned** – given a particular punishment, especially death.

**criminal** – someone who commits a crime.

**deck** – the top outside floor of a boat or ship.

**disease** – a medical condition that causes part of a living thing to no longer work properly.

**flogging** – when a person is hit many times with a whip or stick as a punishment.

**gambling** – playing games of chance or betting on things to try to win money.

**hammocks** – beds made from a net or fabric that are hung up by a string at each end.

**hull** – the main part of a ship at the bottom where it goes in the water.

**imprisonment** – the act of putting someone in prison or jail.

**naval fleets** – groups of ships that a country uses to fight at sea.

**oars** – long poles with a flat, wide blade at one end used for rowing boats.

**planks** – long, narrow, flat pieces of wood.

**license** – to give someone permission to do something.

**licenses** – documents giving someone permission to do something.

**quarters** – rooms that are provided for soldiers, sailors, or servants to live in.

**rigging** – the set of ropes supporting the masts and sails of a ship or boat.

**satchels** – small bags that often have a long strap.

**surrender** – to stop fighting and admit that you have been defeated.

**tar** – a sticky black substance that becomes hard when cool and is used for sealing things.

**rebellion** – when a group of people refuse to follow their leader anymore.

**vessels** – large boats or ships.

# INDEX




Picture credits:

(t=top; b=bottom; m=middle; l=left; r=right):

Shutterstock: Andrey_kuzmin 12bg; Bborris.67 30b; BlackFarm 1bg; Denis---S 10-11bg, 16m; Denys Yelmanov 30tr; Dive.paradise 7tr; Eva Biralūk 4bg; Grafvision 12b; Ilozaur 9tr; JKIWA 15t; Jozef klopacka 13bl; LeStudio 8-9bg; Maradon 333 24m; Muratart 6-7bg; Myotis 27m; Oleksandr_U 19mr; Peyker 9tl; PJ Photography 14bg; Prosign 2-3bg; Rio Adera 5b; Thicaa 26b; VasquezLaboratorium 10bl; Victor Metelskiy 28ml; Zef art 18-19bg. Wikipedia: 13br; 21tl; By Joseph Nicholls (fl. 1726–55).[1] Although James Basire (1730–1802) is attributed as the engraver based on the signature "J. Basire", unless he engraved the item at the age of 6, it is likely his father Isaac Basire (misreading of initial?) or another J. Basire. - http://jcb.lunaimaging.com/luna/servlet/detail/JCB~1~1~1785~2720004:Captain-Teach-commonly-call-d-Black, Public Domain, https://commons.wikimedia.org/w/index.php?curid=159524761 20ml; By Howard Pyle - Pyle, Howard; Johnson, Merle De Vore (ed) (1921) "With the Buccaneers" in Howard Pyle's Book of Pirates: Fiction, Fact & Fancy Concerning the Buccaneers & Marooners of the Spanish Main, New York, United States, and London, United Kingdom: Harper and Brothers, pp. p. 84, Public Domain 21br; By John Michael Wright - Royal Collection RCIN 404951, Public Domain, https://commons.wikimedia.org/w/index.php?curid=42270010 21tr; By Unknown author - http://book.ifeng.com/psl/dzsp/200907/0727_3553_1270289.shtml, Public Domain, https://commons.wikimedia.org/w/index.php?curid=22780504 25tl; By Engraved by Benjamin Cole[2] (1695–1766) - https://americanhistory.si.edu/onthewater/exhibition/1_5.html 22b, 23t; By Paul A. Cziko, CC BY 2.5, https://commons.wikimedia.org/w/index.php?curid=22172272 11mr; By Maurits van Nassau (Maurice of Orange, 1567-1625) / Melander, secretaris - images.nrc.nl. Illustration in article Dutch newspaper NRC 1 January 2020 by Leendert van der Valk: De eerste Afrikaanse Amerikanen werden verhandeld onder de Nederlandse vlag 17b; By User:Fred the Oyster - Angus Konstam, Blackbeard the Pirate, 2007, page 177, CC0, https://commons.wikimedia.org/w/index.php?curid=341073 29tl; By http://www.openclipart.org/cgi-bin/navigate/signs_and_symbols/flags/historic/pirates, CC0, https://commons.wikimedia.org/w/index.php?curid=341043 29bl; By user:EugeneZelenko - Source, CC0, https://commons.wikimedia.org/w/index.php?curid=341064 29br; By Bastianow, CC BY-SA 2.5, https://commons.wikimedia.org/w/index.php?curid=654170 29br;

Every effort has been made to trace the copyright holders, and we apologize in advance for any unintentional omissions. We would be pleased to insert the appropriate acknowledgments in any subsequent edition of this publication.